Horsham and District

IN OLD PHOTOGRAPHS

TONY WALES

Alan Sutton Publishing Limited
Phoenix Mill · Far Thrupp · Stroud
Gloucestershire

First published 1994

Copyright © Tony Wales, 1994

British Library Cataloguing in Publication Data.
A catalogue record for this book is available from
the British Library.

ISBN 0-7509-0757-6

Typeset in 9/10 Sabon.
Typesetting and origination by
Alan Sutton Publishing Limited.
Printed in Great Britain by
The Guernsey Press Company Limited,
Guernsey, Channel Islands.

Horsham and District

IN OLD PHOTOGRAPHS

The well-stocked shop of T. Gillings, fishmonger and poultry seller of East Street, Horsham, Christmas 1906. Mr Gillings (second from left) looks justifiably proud of his shop display, which even includes a swan – at that time these were still considered to be a delicacy. Shops of this sort always made a big effort at Christmas, and it was common for an empty building nearby to be rented for the busy period so that the stock of poultry could be well displayed. On the extreme left is Mr Alf Scott, who subsequently took over the shop in 1937.

Contents

The chemist's shop of R. Gallier on the corner of Horsham's narrowest thoroughfare, Middle Street, in the late nineteenth century. This was once known as Butchers' Row because of the number of butchers' shops in it. Bulls were baited nearby on the Carfax and the carcasses were subsequently brought here to be sold. The meat of the unfortunate bulls was prized, as it was supposed to be particularly tender. Those in favour of the custom said that the bulls enjoyed the 'sport' although no evidence supported this view. The narrowness of the street gave rise to several jokes of the kind enjoyed by nineteenth-century Horsham folk: very fat people were advised not to take this route, and those with long noses were warned against turning their heads. During the Second World War even tanks had to negotiate the street. Now, however, the little road has been pedestrianized.

Introduction

Horsham has changed considerably in the last thirty years or so. Before that, change was much slower, and although my own memories go back to a very different town in the 1920s and '30s, the pace of change was slow enough to be almost imperceptible. In fact I can recall when cattle and sheep were still being driven through the streets, deliveries of many essentials were being made by horse and cart, huge horse-drawn timber wagons lumbered up the Bishopric, and there were still farms alongside town streets. Small locally owned shops made up most of the commercial activity, and little corner shops were open to all hours. There were still itinerent street sellers, offering muffins, hot chestnuts and fruit and vegetables, even on Sundays. These disappeared very gradually, but the Second World War accelerated change, just as the previous war had done.

It is interesting to look back a little further, before my own memories begin, to a time when Horsham was almost self sufficient and the pace of change even slower. Young Howard Dudley, writing in 1836, described the town thus:

> The ancient town and borough of Horsham which has generally been passed over in topographical accounts, as a place unworthy of notice; or lost in dazzling descriptions of the 'modern maritime Babylon of Sussex', must always remain a spot dear to the lover of antiquities and romantic scenery.

Later in his *History and Antiquities of Horsham* he stated:

> Horsham is greatly improving: the number of buildings which have been lately erected, and which are still erecting, are of a new and handsome description: the streets are neatly paved, with the large flat stones procured from the excellent quarries in the neighbourhood; and the illumination of the streets by gas, which is being carried on with great spirit and energy, contribute very greatly to the general respectability and good appearance of the place.

Walser's *Illustrated Guide to Horsham and District* of 1892 is even more complimentary, describing Horsham as 'a thriving and beautiful town; its streets and squares well laid out, and in many places planted with trees; its open spaces numerous'. But of course this was only one side of the coin. Like all towns in the nineteenth century, it was suffering a certain number of growing pains, and there were still eyesores, such as unmade roads, and the lack of what we would now consider essential amenities, like general street lighting and public toilets. But overall it would seem to be a town which was pleased with itself, and changes were not so rapid as to worry the older residents too much.

Although as a boy I was scathing about Horsham's attractions for my own age group (nothing ever changes in this respect), I was still aware that the town had certain things lacking elsewhere, particularly the historical and traditional aspects. As George Aitcheson commented in *Sussex* (1936), 'Horsham has always been a live place, with its own special brands in ghosts, dragons, headless horsemen, smugglers (on a large and prosperous scale), its executions and its famous roofing slabs and its brickfields'.

It is not necessary to go back very far to find traces of these romantic, or should I say barbaric, parts of our local history. For instance it was as recently as the late eighteenth century that the last man was punished at the public whipping post, and it was not until the nineteenth century that bull-baiting on the Carfax came to an end. But slowly these faded into history, and some more pleasant events took place, such as the building of the Carfax bandstand in 1892, and the installation of the first electric street lights in 1902. More recent developments have included the construction of the Davis Estate, built in 1934 on the Jews Meadows, which had long been associated with visiting fairs.

All this is now part of Horsham's historical pageant, and I hope that this collection of old photographs will help to bring the past back to life both for older Horsham residents, and also for the many new residents who have moved into the town. Unlike earlier books, in this one I have been able to extend my excursions into the past, to embrace many of the villages in the Horsham area. Perhaps I should be careful about the use of the word 'villages', as some of these places are now becoming small towns in their own right – although of course they were villages at the time these photographs were taken.

The coverage is unavoidably patchy and no attempt has been made to make the book comprehensive. The selection is based purely on the suitable photographs available, and no slight is intended towards places not represented, or represented rather more briefly than others.

One other explanation regards the grouping of the villages. This is not meant to be geographically exact, but is intended to bring together the villages which seemed to me to belong, or at least to have some affinity, to each other. If my grouping offends anyone, may I apologize here and now.

So here we have it: Horsham and district, warts and all. The pictures go back mainly to the early years of this century, but in a few cases considerably further. I hope it will provide much enjoyment and that my selection of illustrations will give an indication of my affection for the town and the surrounding countryside.

Horsham Carfax at the turn of the century. Once this had been a green open space, occupied at certain times of the year by fairs and the like. Even when it had become built up, it remained the hub of the town, and the townsfolk's favourite meeting-place. The splendid edifice in the foreground of this picture is the drinking fountain erected to commemorate Queen Victoria's Diamond Jubilee in 1897 (see p. 63). During my own childhood, it was often used by thirsty children, although I was always admonished not to drink from the metal cup used by all and sundry.

The Carfax bandstand was built in 1891 on the site used for bonfires on 5 November. In my mother's teenage years, the young people, discreetly separated, used to parade around the stand while the band played, always hoping that one of the boys would pluck up the courage to ask one of the girls to walk home with him. The scene would have been very different earlier in the nineteenth century: each July the annual Pleasure Fair was held, with its booths, sideshows and gypsys' vans.

Another view of the Carfax, early 1900s. As well as the drinking fountain and the bandstand, the Stout House (centre, right), one of half a dozen Carfax pubs, is in view. North Street (just visible behind the tree) began at the north-east corner, and St Mark's Church, built in 1840 as a chapel-of-ease to the parish church, can be seen in the background. By this time it had its familiar spire, although originally it was built without one.

Horsham stocks, on the Carfax, in the early part of this century. By this time they were merely a curiosity, although a century earlier they would have been in use as a punishment for minor offences such as drunkenness. They were apparently rediscovered in 1859 and two 'volunteers' were persuaded to try them for size. A postcard of this event, produced later, stated that the stocks then disappeared again, and had possibly been burnt on a bonfire for 5 November. However, the originals (or duplicates) appear to have survived and they were certainly in daily view on the Carfax during my own childhood. These are now safe in Horsham Museum and a replica set may be seen in a slightly different spot on the Carfax, together with a replica of the old whipping post.

The 'King's Head Corner' early this century, with the old inscription 'Revenue Office' on the front of the building. The inscription dates from the late nineteenth century, when the Inland Revenue had an office here. The building itself is a fifteenth-century coaching hotel, which had its own stables up to about the time of this picture. It also operated a horse bus to the railway station, and had its own assembly rooms, once Horsham's only 'theatre'. In my own youth, this corner was usually controlled by a policeman, although I can remember the rare occasion when an AA Scout (as they were

called) was pressed into service. Middle Street is on the left, and although it was very narrow it was open to vehicles, which were expected to pass in both directions. Fortunately there was little traffic, but when, as sometimes happened, two carters with their horses met face to face, it was a question of who had the loudest voice and the most compelling will, as to which one would give way. For many years there was a chemist's on this corner, at one time owned by R. Gallier, then E.A. Kittle (as seen here), and latterly H.R. Camplin.

Lintott's, the well-known local wholesale grocer's at 10 the Carfax. The premises were dated 1841 but they are seen here just before these buildings were demolished, to be replaced by a row of shops known as Sterling Buildings. This took place in 1938, and crowds watched in awe as Lintott's familiar chimney was pulled down by chains fixed to a steam traction engine. One of the distinctive Carfax lamp standards can be seen on the traffic island in the foreground. These handsome lamps were said to be the brainchild of Councillor Mrs Nellie (Vesta) Laughton, a Horsham celebrity of that time.

Hunt Brothers' drapery shop at 1, 2 and 3 West Street. This picture is taken from Walser's *Illustrated Guide to Horsham and District* (1892), and shows a certain amount of artistic licence in making the premises look larger and grander than in reality. But then Hunt Brothers' shop was always considered to be one of the premier businesses in Horsham, and those who were fortunate enough to work there felt they were a cut above mere draper's assistants, not least because the shop closed at midday on Saturdays. In 1892 the business claimed that it had been established nearly a century, so perhaps they had good reason to feel a trifle superior. The building was demolished in 1906, and the site was sold to the Capital and Counties Bank. The proceeds of the sale allowed Hunt Brothers to build a new shop, which was later replaced by the Seeboard showroom. The corner site is still occupied by a bank, but it is now Lloyds.

A rather amateurish photograph, from the late nineteenth or early twentieth century, of Farley & Co. at 50 West Street. Originally Farley's sold corn, seed, hay, feed and manure. Later it also became a baker's, specializing in Prewett's Millstone flour and bread, and a café. Farley's is usually claimed to have the oldest shop front in Horsham. Like the picture below there appears to be a call for celebration when the photograph was taken.

S. Price's shop at 48 West Street, shown on an undated postcard. The decorations suggest 1897, the year of Queen Victoria's Diamond Jubilee, or perhaps they were for a subsequent coronation. The business was founded by Sydney Price in 1848, and remained in the same premises until its closure in 1956. Their advertising described them as 'Stationers, Booksellers, Printers, Bookbinders, Newsagents, suppliers of Artist's Requisites, and Circulating Library. Printers for the Italian Ambassador, and the Collyer's School Magazine.'

A delightful photograph of H. Churchman's, grocer's and provision merchant's, at the turn of the century. The shop was on the corner of Middle Street and South Street; in the 1920s it was taken over by Evershed and Cripps, although to older Horsham folk it was still known as Churchman's right up to modern times when it ceased to be a grocer's shop. Before this, it was probably Horsham's last specialist grocer's shop. The staff seen here show great pride in their calling. Note the tantalizing prices of the goods on sale. The hoist in the doorway of the upper warehouse was in constant use to haul boxes and barrels up and down from the carts below, and was a great attraction to all the young lads like myself in the 1930s. Another enjoyable sight each December was the masses of Christmas crackers displayed in the window on the left. No shop in Horsham had such a selection or such expensive ones. Of course, it was purely a question of looking, rather than actually buying.

Opposite: H. Churchman's advertisement in Walser's *Illustrated Guide to Horsham and District*. It filled a complete page of the guide and was obviously intended to stress the importance of this well-known Horsham business. Comparing the artist's drawing with the actual shop shown opposite one can see that he erred on the side of generosity in the size of the building compared to the diminutive figures on the pavement and roadway. Nevertheless it is a lovely drawing, particularly the illustration of the hoist in use. The text gives a very good idea of the kind of stock carried by the shop, although what was meant by the phrase 'co-operative prices charged for cash', one can but surmise.

H. CHURCHMAN,

⁓ GROCER, ⁓

Provision, Wine, Spirit, Ale, Stout & Mineral Water

MERCHANT,

SOUTH ✝ STREET, ✝ HORSHAM.

Foreign and British Cigars.

EGYPTIAN CIGARETTES AND FANCY TOBACCOS.

PRICE LISTS FREE.

CO-OPERATIVE PRICES CHARGED FOR CASH.

Timothy White's in West Street, July 1929. It was a chemist's but, rather like Boots today, also stocked a large range of other goods. Its advertisements mentioned such things as 'All the latest novels' and even 'wire netting'. Later it joined forces with another well-known firm and became Timothy White and Taylor. The group outside gives some idea of the size of the staff in 1929. It includes C. Gumbrell, Ivy Holmes, Phyllis Cob, Win Lucas, Gladys Champion (from Southwater), Milly Barnard and Ethel Potter. I wonder who had the unenviable job of taking down all those baths and buckets each night, and hanging them up again the following morning.

West Street, *c.* 1906. The tall man in the foreground appears to be parading down the street, and I would hazard a guess that he is a 'giant', probably from 'Lord' George Sangers' visiting circus. Also in the picture is a porter's trolley, which appears to be filled with cases belonging to a travelling salesman. In the days before almost everyone owned a car, the salesmen would visit different towns by train, using the services of a railway porter to transport their wares to the shops they wished to visit. Cecil Cramp's father recalled one such salesman, accompanied by a trolley loaded with suitcases, looking forlornly at a deserted West Street on a Thursday afternoon (unlike most towns, with half-day closing on Wednesdays, Horsham always closed its shops on Thursdays). Also visible here, in a shop window, is a poster advertising the impending opening of Timothy White's shop.

Looking west along a busy West Street, early 1900s. At that time it was said that the clock on the right always stood at 8.55. Hunt Brothers' shop is prominent on the left, and Jury Cramp's famous spectacles can also be seen on the left. He moved from Middle Street to West Street in 1878.

A window display at Woolworths Threepenny and Sixpenny Store at 45 West Street, 1936. Woolworths provided a real service to its customers, offering thousands of items, many of them very small and unimportant, but all under sixpence each. However, it has to be mentioned that sometimes very subtle means were employed to stick with this policy. For instance, it was possible to buy a camera costing half a crown but one received it in five sixpenny sections. At least it made the replacement of any broken bits very simple and inexpensive. My own memories of pre-war 'Woollies' are all pleasant ones, and they received a good proportion of my pocket money. This was particularly so at Christmas when the outing to buy my family's presents was carried out entirely in the Threepenny and Sixpenny Store.

John Stanford's pram and cycle shop at 49 East Street, Horsham, early this century. This was next to the Primitive Methodist Chapel, later known as the Fellowship Hall. The shop itself became Lovett's the greengrocer's by the 1930s. Like many cycle shops at that time, the business was changing to include motor cycles, and a notice suggested customers 'Fill up here', which evidently referred to petrol. Stanford's was not entirely devoted to things mechanical, however, as shown by the wooden toy horses at the front of the shop.

Opposite: One of several grocery shops in West Street, almost certainly the Maypole Store at no. 46, next to Woolworths, *c*. 1937. My mother did her weekly shopping here, and as a boy I have vivid memories of the manager of the shop patting up the butter on the counter with tremendous aplomb, ending with the Maypole insignia on the top of the pat. The family must have used the shop (or an earlier version at a different site on the other side of West Street) for a long time, as the story was told by my aunt of the day when my great-grandmother went into the shop and slipped and fell flat on the floor. When an assistant tried to help her up, she brushed him aside with the immortal remark 'Young man, how much is your shilling-a-pound butter?' This, I was assured, was perfectly typical of Grandma.

The drapery and millinery shop of C.A. Phillips in East Street, *c.* 1910. Like all such shops at this time, the windows were packed with goods, and removing and replacing the goods displayed must have taken the shop assistant at least a couple of days, even without interruptions. Seen here, left to right: Mrs Phillips, Dorothy Tyhurst, Mrs Brackpool, Miss Boyce.

The yard at the back of Jackson's shop at 43 West Street, probably in the 1920s. Originally Jackson's had been bicycle makers, but later became motor engineers with works in Springfield and London Road. As I remember it, the West Street shop was invariably full of bicycles of all shapes and sizes awaiting repair. It offered a very useful and quick service, and was sandwiched rather incongruously between a hosiery shop (Hawkins') and a ladies hairdresser's (Slade-Symes').

A picture from 1908 of the Primitive Methodist Chapel in East Street, which had been built in 1891. In 1932 the churches of the Primitive Methodists and the Wesleyan Methodists amalgamated and the East Street Chapel closed down. It then became the Fellowship Hall, which thrived from the 1930s onwards. The premises were also used by other organizations such as the International Friendship League. It is now the Horsham Christian Live Centre.

The fire at the Horsham tannery, *c.* 1912. The frame of the building was cast in London in 1842, and it is said that it spent the first fifty years of its existence as a tannery building in Bermondsey, which was then the centre of the tanning industry. It was removed and re-erected in Horsham around 1880 or 1890.

Another picture of the aftermath of the fire, at what became known as the Brighton Road Tanyard Depot. The building was originally open sided, with the hides suspended inside. In the 1930s it became part of a West Sussex County Council yard, which was not needed when a new depot was opened at Broadbridge Heath. In this picture the boys seem more interested in the photographer than in the result of the fire.

An early nineteenth-century picture of Sussex County Gaol on the north side of East Street. One of many Horsham gaols, it was built between 1775 and 1779 at a cost of £3,560, to plans prepared by the Duke of Richmond. It was said to be a great improvement on previous gaols and when the prison reformer John Howard visited it in 1782 he remarked that it was 'as quiet as a private house'. Also noteworthy is that in 1844 John Lawrence was executed for murder on a scaffold erected beside the gaol; this was the last public hanging in Horsham and was witnessed by an estimated 3,000 people. The building was sold in 1845 to Henry Michell, who demolished it, to make use of its 2½ million bricks, 15,000 ft of Horsham paving stone, 100 doors and 150 windows. Some of these materials turned up in other Horsham buildings which he erected.

The Baptist Chapel in Queen Street, early 1900s. After meetings had been held in other Nonconformist churches in Horsham, the local Baptists held a service in the King's Head Assembly Rooms in 1894 and decided to build their own chapel. Originally it had an iron roof with a brick frontage, and when it rained services were interrupted by the noise of the water on the metal roof. In 1923 a new building was erected on the same site. The opening service was followed by teas which cost 9d per person. In 1994 the Horsham Baptist Church is proudly celebrating its centenary.

The Causeway and the parish church of St Mary the Virgin, around the turn of the century. There was originally a Norman church on the north bank of the River Arun. This was demolished, and parts of it were incorporated into a new building, possibly around 1247. Additions and alterations were made in subsequent centuries, with major changes between 1864 and 1865. The result is a noble building, whose splendid spire can be seen from Denne Hill to the south. Like some other famous spires it is slightly out of true, leaning a little to the south-west, apparently due to the action of the sun on the wooden shingles. The Causeway was once maintained by the church authorities, as a main route between the centre of the town and the church. In the late nineteenth century a 'Jack o' the Clock' figure dressed in scarlet and gold, which struck the hours and quarters, was removed from the west end of the church. The reason given was that it disturbed the worshippers and was expensive to maintain.

The tree-lined Causeway, looking north towards the back of the Town Hall, in the late nineteenth century. Previously spelt in several ways, such as Casey and Causy, this has remained one of Horsham's most attractive thoroughfares, leading to St Mary's, the Arun and Denne Hill. In my mother's childhood it was an unmade road, with stepping stones at certain points to enable walkers to cross easily on wet and muddy days. Although today the buildings are all uncommercial, she recalled how a regular errand was to go to a house in the Causeway which sold, among other things, loose pickles. For these one needed an empty basin, and when this was filled, my mother would carefully take it home, only pausing occasionally to sample the pickles which lay temptingly in the open receptacle.

St Mary's Church from the east, late nineteenth century. One of the most notable events in its 800-year history took place in 1830 when a mob marched on Horsham, and demanded a meeting with the magistrates and the vicar in the old church. Horsham's most important man at that time, Mr Hurst, refused to attend, but the crowd grabbed a carriage from the King's Head and threatened to take him there by force if necessary. He then agreed to come in his own carriage. By this time the rioters were tearing up the church railings, and shouting for the vicar to be burned. Then Mr Lee mounted the communion table, and persuaded them to listen to the vicar, who agreed to take a 10 per cent cut in his tithes. As wiser counsels prevailed, the labourers dispersed. The following day Mr Hurst ordered that fifty or sixty men be sworn in as town constables, but public sympathy was so much with the rioters that only two could be found willing to serve.

A peaceful view of St Mary's and the Garden of Remembrance, provided in 1930 by Mrs Nellie (Vesta) Laughton, in memory of her late husband and others who died in the First World War. Things were not always quite so tranquil here, however. In the eighteenth century prisoners from the gaol were obliged to attend services in the church, and a letter from 1749 paints a grim picture: 'The six smugglers that are to be executed in a few days, come to church every time there is a service. Their melancholy looks (for they seem to behave very suitably to their condition) and the clanking of their chains, make it so disagreeable, I wonder the people can bear it. For they stand in the middle aisle where it is almost impossible to avoid looking at them.'

The placid and peaceful infant River Arun, which rises in St Leonard's Forest close to Horsham, early this century. The date of the footbridge is uncertain. It probably replaced a stone causeway, though there may have been other footbridges before the present one. This leads from the churchyard across to the cricket ground, known before the last century as Barrack Fields or the Artillery Ground.

The early days of Horsham's Garden of Remembrance, sited in what had been known as Mill Bay. It cost £300, which was a small fortune then, and was landscaped with seats, a bandstand, and play facilities for children. Mrs Laughton offered the gardens to the Council but it was unwilling to take on their upkeep. When she died in 1953 at the age of eighty-three the Council did take over the gardens, although they were poorly maintained. In recent years the Horsham Society, with other help, has done a tremendous amount to improve the area, and the Council now looks after it properly.

The children's paddling-pool in the Garden of Remembrance, with the church behind. The pool no longer exists. The benefactor, councillor and JP Mrs Laughton was also a local 'character'. Always dressed in flowing outfits of black and white, she loved to make her way down the street talking to everyone and dispensing lumps of sugar to the tradesmen's horses. When she was on the bench, she would sometimes take pity on the accused and pay the fine from her own capacious handbag, but she was generous, too, in much bigger ways: the town's first ambulance was purchased by her.

Denne Park House early this century. Standing a short distance to the south of Horsham, on the top of a picturesque hill, the name Denne or Dane, with the adjacent Picts Hill, ties in with the tradition that there was once a camp of Danish warriors here, arming themselves against Alfred the Great. The Elizabethan house overlooks the beautiful park, which has been enjoyed by the inhabitants of the town for a very long time. The ground at the top of the hill was once kept mown and rolled, forming a fine promenade, which was enjoyed by young ladies and their escorts on summer evenings.

This lovely avenue of lime trees leads from Worthing Road to the deer park of Denne. It is pictured around the turn of the century, when Denne Park was particularly popular with local folk on a fine summer evening. The view overlooking the town, river and church at the foot of the hill is particularly striking. It is said that the original iron gates of the mansion were brought from Chesworth and that the Elizabethan mansion of Denne was erected in its place, when Chesworth was falling into disrepair.

Rice Bros' car showroom, Worthing Road, 1921. The firm started up in 1895, with a shop in West Street, and was originally a saddlery and harness maker's. It also produced bicycles, and these eventually became the main part of the enterprise. The West Street premises suffered a bad fire in 1909, but from 1899 the firm was also operating a coachbuilding business in Springfield Road. In addition, a car showroom was opened around 1913 in Worthing Road; this eventually became Gilbert Rice's – the change of name was used to maintain the Ford agency, while different makes were sold in the firm's other premises. The handsome archway in this picture was said to have been constructed from materials taken from the old gaol in East Street, when it was bought by Henry Michell in 1845. Other bits of the prison were used in the new police station, and in railway works.

Worthing Road, looking north, *c.* 1910. At that time it was a quiet country lane, seen here with two cyclists, rather than the busy main road it is today. The photographer has been lucky enough to catch a group of dandies, including one with a straw boater, so popular at that period. Also in the picture is William Prewett's Mill and Engineering Works at Mill Bay Lane. Prewett advertised himself as 'Miller, Corn Merchant, Engineer to the Automobile Club, Motor, Electrical and General Engineer, Millwright and Agricultural Machinist' (they didn't go in for undue modesty in advertising at that time). Mill Bay Lane provided a favourite local walk, leading to the Arun and back through the churchyard. Near here is the roadbridge across the river; a bridge has existed here in different forms since the seventeenth century. The present bridge dates from 1924 when the road was widened.

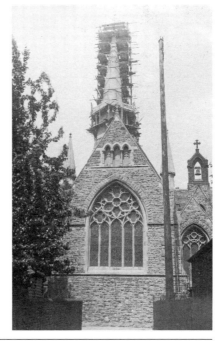

An unusual view of St Mark's Church in North Street, showing the spire encased in scaffolding, 1920s. The church was designed by the Sussex architect, E.P. Loftus Brock, and was built without a spire; this was added later as a memorial to a local canon's daughter. In 1989 the decision was made to demolish the church, although the 142 ft tower and spire remained. Eleven thousand people had signed a petition to save the building, and the Victorian Society took the case to the High Court. But it was all in vain, and the much-loved building disappeared as part of the Horsham redevelopment scheme of the 1980s.

Reminiscent of a Christmas card scene is this view of the junction of North Street and Park Street, *c.* 1910. St Mark's spire is behind, shrouded in mist. Many will remember the shop in the centre (left) as Model Corner, owned by Dennis Childs until its demolition in 1988. Older Horsham folk will recall when it was the corn chandler's, run by the Chart family. Amos 'Father' Chart was a well-known local figure, much loved by the children, especially when he cleaned out his coal cart to transport them on their Sunday school outings.

A painting of the medieval houses in North Street as they appeared in the 1900s. These were roughly opposite Amos Chart's corn business. When they had been pulled down, one part of the houses was re-erected as Fullers next to the golf course at Mannings Heath, in the 1920s.

Next to the cottages were the carriage builders Bailey Bros. Earlier the business had been called Ward & Thorn, which still existed in 1903, so this picture must have been taken some time after this. Later the business changed to Eric L. Carr, automobile engineers, surely a most apt name. Later it became Rowland & Page's engineering works, and ultimately Caffyn's garage.

Dunkin's typewriter shop in North Street, next to J.C. Padwick's house (a local JP), 1930s. This photograph was taken with a Baby Brownie camera by local photographer Alfred Hills. Dunkin's is typical of the time when Horsham was still a town of mainly small, locally owned businesses, many of them the only one of their kind. At that time Dunkin's was *the* shop for typewriters, duplicators and office supplies. Mr Dunkin had taken over the shop from Renwick & Co. and, as I well remember, he was always ready with helpful information and advice for his customers, most of whom were also his friends.

A rather amateur photograph from around 1908, of Denman's baker's and confectioner's at 39 North Street. Like many such businesses it also functioned as a café, although many local people will remember it better as Erridge's baker's shop in more recent years. Surprisingly the building still survives, in spite of the chaos of redevelopment which surrounded it in the late 1980s.

North Street, looking towards the railway station, *c.* 1921. One of Horsham's famous ornate lamp-posts is to the right. There are also cows placidly grazing on the grass verge – not an uncommon site even as late as the 1920s. The few cars around just had to put up with them. On the left is the wall of Park House. At about that time there was talk of lowering this, to improve the view across the park from the road, but it was not done.

Opposite: Horsham Fire Engine Station in North Street, next to Henry Smith, the auctioneers, *c.* 1912. Before the brigade was formed, 'Old Ike' (Isaac Aldridge, a local carpenter) was in charge of the engine, which was presented to the town in 1780 by Lady Irwin of Hills Place. It was stored in a shed, and it took him forty-five minutes to get it into working order when needed. Fortunately, the Horsham Volunteer Fire Brigade was formed in 1840. This included a captain, lieutenant, four superintendents, salvage and escape foremen, four engineers, twelve firemen and three messengers. The firemen, who were local tradesmen, wore pot hats, and were very proud of their turnout. The brigade was taken over by the Horsham Urban District Council in 1911.

TELEPHONE: HORSHAM 16,

From F. ROBERTS, STATION HOTEL, HORSHA

AMILY AND COMMERCIAL.   MOTOR GARAGE.   CARS ON HIRE.   SOLE AGENT L. B.

An advertising card for Frederick Roberts, who ran the Station Hotel and posting house, *c.* 1910. This stood opposite Horsham station which was operated by the London Brighton & South Coast Railway company. As the number of cars increased Mr Roberts extended his hotel business to include a motor garage, which also hired cars. In addition he was proud to claim a sole agency for the railway. Another of his claims at that time was that the hotel was 'fitted throughout with electric lights'. He had the low telephone number of 16, so presumably he was one of Horsham's earlierst subscribers. By the 1930s other proprietors had replaced him, but the phone number remained 16.

Opposite: The staff stand outside Mrs Elizabeth Seagrave's bakery at the corner of Springfield Road and the Bishopric, in the late nineteenth century. Seagrave's was a high-class bakery, and the scent of its bread early in the morning gave an intimation of the pleasures to come. As the picture shows this was an old-fashioned shop, and it recalled the days not so long before, when normal closing hours were as late as 8 p.m. in the summer and 7 p.m. in winter. Bakers and similar shops were open on Sundays at least until the church service. Many will remember Piggott's fine ironmonger's and household stores, which occupied this site in the 1930s.

North Parade around 1910 was (and still is) an attractive tree-lined road leading out of the town towards London. Springfield Park is on one side and Hurst (later Horsham) Park is on the other. Most pictures taken from this viewpoint (Potter's Corner) are similar, irrespective of their date, but this one has an attractive lamp standard in the foreground which is not usually seen. North Parade was the usual route for the many people living in the 'Common' area of Horsham to reach the town, at least until the Davis Estate was built; this extended Rushams Road to the Bishopric. As a child it seemed a very long route, particularly on Sundays when I walked it with my parents at least twice in each direction to attend church. Now it seems much shorter.

Springfield Road, c. 1910. This was known earlier as Chapel Lane, following the purchase by John Morth of a cottage to be used as a chapel for the Society of Independents. It was once an important road to London, and was turnpiked in 1755 – a very unpopular action much resented by the townsfolk. On the left of this picture are the railings of the Roman Catholic School, which was endowed by the Duke of Norfolk. Miss Eleanor Marsh was the formidable headmistress at this time, known always as 'Governess'. On the right are the railings of the Congregational Chapel, built on Swan Meadow which was owned by the duke. The chapel was removed and completely rebuilt in 1982. On either side were two short roads, Albion Terrace and Albion Road, linking Springfield Road with the Carfax.

Opposite: The Meter Room at the Horsham Gas Works – an unlikely subject for a photograph, probably taken around 1920. The works were between Springfield Road and London Road, and were completed in 1839. The gas company had been formed in 1835, and a year later gas lighting first appeared in the town. One of the last major buildings to be lit by gas was the railway station, which still had this mellow form of lighting long after other public buildings had changed to electricity. (Now some of the town lighting is again provided by gas.) The gas works closed in the 1950s, and were finally demolished in 1959. It was while workmen were engaged on this task that a tunnel was discovered running under Springfield Road to what had once been fields on the opposite side. This was linked to the smuggling of illicit malt, said to have been operated from one of the buildings in the area.

The owners and staff of Jackson Bros motor-car business, situated between London Road and Springfield Road, c. 1905. The two lovely old cars are a Humber and a Clement Talbot. The premises were close to the corner which is still often referred to as Potter's Corner, after a former local shopkeeper. Jackson's took over a school building and a foundry, but the site is now occupied by a rather strange star-shaped office block.

A print of the Royal British Schools at the north end of London Road, which were taken over by Jackson's garage in the 1900s. The foundry and its chimney can be seen on the left. The schools were in London Road from 1814, although they were rebuilt in 1826. Their rules stated that education was to be provided for poor children aged seven to thirteen of all religious denominations, and reading lessons were to come only from Scripture. A fee of tuppence ha'penny a week was charged to parents who could afford to pay it.

Springfield Park House, pictured early this century, was built in 1789 by the Blunt family. The grounds around the house were noted for their fine trees, which included specimens of the Cedar of Lebanon.

Horsham's Regency Terrace, Brunswick Place in London Road, early this century. It was built in 1835, around the same time as the original Methodist Chapel. This was replaced by the present church, which can be seen on the left and which dates from 1882. Many of the bricks and other materials from the first building were used in the new church. A newspaper report of the opening gave the following information: 'The interior is both cheerful and comfortable, and is fitted with the most modern improvements in lighting, ventilation etc. The seats which are easy and comfortable are arranged to accommodate a congregation of 420.'

'Dad' White of Pondtail Road, c. 1859. He was a founder member of the firm of Grist & Steel and a colour sergeant of the Salvation Army. He is standing beside the rather grim-looking exterior of the first Horsham Salvation Army Citadel in Springfield Road, next to Jackson Bros' motor works. Unfortunately the photographer forgot to tell him to stand completely still, and he has ended up looking a trifle ethereal.

Hedger's shoeing and jobbing smithy in London Road, early 1900s. This was one of many smithies in Horsham and lasted longer than most. Even in the 1930s, when I was a schoolboy, I was fascinated on many occasions to see a horse's head protruding from the half-door. The buildings on the left were known as Mr Mill's cottages.

William Shaw, the wheelwright in London Road, *c.* 1900. Also in this picture is the baker's cart from Mrs Seagrave's shop on the corner of Springfield Road and the Bishopric (see p. 39). Next to Shaw's was J. Penfold's jobbing smithy. In 1907 Shaw's became Spooner & Gordon, and the tenancy agreement still exists between Thomas Spooner, R.W. Gordon and the Hurst Estate, which owned the property until 1950. The complete building was carefully taken down and has now been reassembled at the Amberley Chalk Pits Museum, where it can be seen occupied by craftsmen working in the traditional ways.

Horsham Cottage Hospital in Hurst Road. It was built in 1890 and is seen here early this century. The town had badly needed its own hospital, and so the Vicar of Horsham called a public meeting to raise funds. The hospital cost £1,950 and was formally opened on Saturday 2 July 1892. In January 1922 plans for a new, larger hospital were prepared. The cottage hospital closed on 26 May 1923 after a useful life of thirty-one years, and was sold for £2,500. In 1975 the original building again became part of Horsham Hospital and is now known as The Hospital Annexe.

Collyer's (Horsham Grammar School) in Hurst Road, early 1900s. Named after its founder Richard Collyer, the school started up in 1541 on a site near the parish church. This building was demolished in 1840 and a new school was built in Denne Road. It moved to Hurst Road in 1893. During the interwar years, the road was noted for its uniformed grammar school boys, especially the prefects with their tassled caps, and the fact that the boys always used the pavement on one side of the road only. The school became a sixth-form college in 1976.

South of the centre of Horsham is the area known as Tower Hill; in my mother's time it was a popular destination for a Sunday afternoon walk, along the attractive stone-paved pathway from Worthing Road. When Lady Hurst wrote her book on Horsham in 1868, she mentioned a tradition of a tower which once stood here. There is in fact evidence that a tower existed in 1824, and local historian Frank Holmes believes this tower must have been pulled down before Lady Hurst's time. Sometime after 1870 a newer, smaller tower was built, but why or by whom we know not, although it has been suggested that it was to enable a local landowner to spy on his workforce. This must be the tower in this picture which dates from early in the century. It was about 18 ft high, probably much smaller than the original edifice. During the First World War Charles Marsh worked as a temporary master at Christ's Hospital School nearby. He retired at the end of the war, and built a house in this area. He was annoyed by the Victorian tower, which obscured his view over Horsham, and he had it pulled down and sold the bricks. Or so the story goes!

Townsfolk

A steam lorry and its driver, *c.* 1932. The lorry was owned by the well-known Horsham firm of H. Kay Ltd, which had its depot in Stanley Street. Although by this time steam was reluctantly giving way to petrol for even heavy carrying jobs, vehicles like this were still a familiar sight on the Horsham roads. Another picture in my collection shows a whole fleet owned by Kays, including four steam-engines, two steamrollers and just one motor lorry. As a schoolboy at that time, I was fascinated by the steam monsters, and couldn't imagine that the time would come when they might be considered collectable antiques.

William Law, Horsham's champion town crier. He gained his title at the National Town Crier's Championship at Devizes, in 1912. On his return to Horsham he was ceremoniously carried from the station to the Carfax bandstand; there he was applauded by the townsfolk, who had turned out in force to greet their hero. But not everyone was in awe of his grand appearance. My mother recalled how she and her school friends would follow him around the town, calling out 'Billy La La' in imitation of his own mighty tones. Billy was the last of a line of Horsham town criers. After his time, the office lapsed and eventually his bell and other items passed into the keeping of Horsham Museum.

A picture of the Horsham Town Crier's bell taken by a local photographer in the early 1900s. Although not formally granted to the town until 1944, the Horsham crest of a rather mild-looking lion can be seen on the bell. The official description is a 'lion rampant' and it was first used in the late 1800s. It was derived from the arms of the De Braose and Mowbray families, Lords of the Manor in the Middle Ages.

This fine Father Christmas-like character was Mr G. Scutt of 26 Causeway. He was a member of the Horsham Volunteer Fire Brigade and is pictured in 1840. Unofficial members were often recruited by the Fire Chief, Captain Honeywood, who believed in involving the public as much as possible. On drill nights he would persuade as many onlookers as possible to stand in two lines opposite the fire station. Buckets were then passed from hand to hand down one line and returned along the other.

The Wesley Guild Orchestra, c. 1898. The Wesley Guild is still very much alive and meets fortnightly during the winter in the London Road Wesley Hall, beside the Horsham Methodist Church. The orchestra was in existence for a number of years, sometimes playing for the Sunday service in the church. In one of the front rows of solid wooden pews there was a seat which could be lifted up to give the conductor more space. The first Wesleyan chapel was built in 1832, and the later church in 1883; many additions to the buildings were made over the years. Local church life has always been rich in groups and clubs, which even the cinema and television have failed to destroy.

St John's Roman Catholic Primary School and pupils in Springfield Road, Horsham, c. 1884. The school was erected by the Duke of Norfolk and was close to the site of the present-day Catholic church. However, it was removed to make way for a church hall and car park, during the first phase of modern redevelopment.

Roman Catholic priest Father Munroe, with his choir and altar boys, c. 1900. Fr Munroe came to Horsham in 1879, and died not very long after this picture was taken. He was a popular pastor, not least because of his skills as an amateur conjuror. The building in the background is the original RC church, which was on the east side of Springfield Road. It was built in 1865 and was last used in 1919, when the present church was opened on the opposite side of the road.

Will and May, a Horsham wedding couple captured for posterity by local photographer Mr Waller. All we know is that the date was 25 March 1918. Even a reproduction of this picture in a Sussex newspaper failed to jog anyone's memory as to the identity of Will and May, or their subsequent history. Now that the photograph has appeared in this book, perhaps someone will recall a relative of this name. . . . If so, I would love to hear from them.

This fine old gentleman wielding the pump handle is Mr (Nicholas?) Voice, outside his house at 6 North Street, c. 1904. The Voices were an old Horsham family, well known for their patent blind and cornice works in North Street, and later in Wickersham Road.

Some of the lads of the 1st Horsham Company of the Boys Life Brigade, *c.* 1910. The brigade was attached to Horsham Wesleyan Church (now the Methodist church) in London Road. Their first and only captain was David Lewry, who was remembered by his 'boys' with tremendous affection. The brigade met first in a room in Albion Road and then in the stable yard of Mr Lewry's shop, opposite the Wesleyan chapel. Boys joined at the age of ten and left at nineteen, paying a small weekly sub. Activities included gymnastics, band practice, first aid and flag signalling; the only compulsory activity was the drill parade on Thursday evenings. My father's own favourite was the annual summer camp.

Sussex Volunteers outside the old Drill Hall in Park Street, Horsham, *c.* 1890. (The hall burnt down, was rebuilt and then demolished in the first Horsham redevelopment.) The 1st Battalion of the Royal Sussex Regiment served in the South African War, and was reinforced by the militia. Three successive companies were formed from the volunteer units of the regiment (the first time that the Volunteers had served overseas). In 1908 the Territorial Army was formed out of the volunteer forces with the 4th Battalion in West Sussex and the 5th in East Sussex.

An excellent portrait of the 5th Horsham Brownie Pack in 1923, by local photographer E.W. Copnall. This pack disbanded in the 1930s, but another 5th Horsham pack now exists, although they look a little different from the girls in this picture. The archive section of The Girl Guide Association tells me that the Brown Owl here was Miss D. Munro-Higgs and the Tawny Owl was Miss B. Munro-Higgs. Many people will remember the family and their connections with education in Horsham. Another point of interest is the fine (presumably) stuffed owl in the centre.

Horsham Town Band, 1905. This band was formed in the early nineteenth century and played at the coronation celebrations of Queen Victoria in 1838. In his *Reminiscences of Horsham* Henry Burstow states that the band's favourite tunes were 'Hearts of Oak', 'Bonnie Dundee', 'Bonnets of Blue', 'Rory O'More', and 'Brighton Camp'. The band was the forerunner of Horsham's present-day Royal British Legion Concert Band.

An undated photograph of Horsham Recreation Silver Band, which was formed around 1900. The conductor was Mr H. Bampton. One of the musicians and an enthusiastic supporter was Mr William Albery, who later became Horsham's best-known historian.

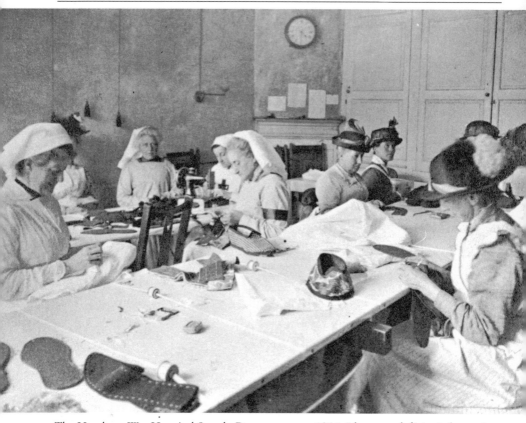

The Horsham War Hospital Supply Department, *c.* 1915. I have no definite information on the location, but it was probably in the building just to the north of Horsham Museum, in the Causeway. Note that the non-nursing helpers have been careful to keep their hats on, as of course this was a period when no self-respecting lady was ever seen hatless outside her own home.

SECTION THREE

Celebrations and Special Events

The Wednesday market in the Bishopric. Farmers drove into the town from miles around in their dog-carts and wagonettes, and the boys were happy to help mind the cattle in exchange for a penny as payment. Sometimes the market became a fair, with swingboats and roundabouts in the Jews Meadows at one end of the Bishopric. Gypsies showed off their horses up and down Worthing Road, and the Bishopric cobblestones were covered with stalls selling all kinds of cheap but desirable items. The local schools sometimes had difficulty keeping up their attendances on fair days. Early this century the market became too much for what was becoming a busy main road into the town, and it moved to the railway station goods yard – but it was never quite the same.

A memento of the Black Horse Hotel, at the corner of West Street and Worthing Road. Known affectionately as 'The Old Kicker', it was a well-established Horsham landmark dating back to the early nineteenth century. Next to it was the Corn Exchange, built in 1866 at a cost of £4,000. This was incorporated into the hotel in 1913, and the complete complex was demolished in the 1960s, to make way for shops. The hotel was well known even up to my own childhood for its election dinners, balls and other social events. Undoubtedly some of its earlier success was due to its connections with the local farmers through the adjoining Corn Exchange, and there was once a weekly poultry market held in the hotel itself.

The recasting of the bells of St Mary the Virgin, in the Causeway. The date may be 1890, or perhaps 1921 (when the bells and frames were restored and three bells recast). The date of Horsham's earliest bells is not known, but there were six in use up to 1752, when a further two were added. The curfew was rung from the church daily until 1891. Probably the occasion which sparks off memories for many folk is the pealing of the bells at midnight on New Year's Eve. One year it was touch-and-go as to whether the peal would be sounded at all, as the ringers were at loggerheads. The troubles were eventually settled by one of the wives and the men all tiptoed from the Talbot to ring in the New Year. Henry Burstow was able to claim that he had taken part in ringing the old year out in Horsham for sixty-five years without a break.

A

GENUINE ACCOUNT

O F

ANNE WHALE and *SARAH PLEDGE*,

Who were tried and condemned at the Affizes held at *Hor-fham* in the County of *Suffex*,

Before the Right Honble Sir JOHN WILLES, Lord Chief Juftice of his Majefty's Court of *Common Pleas*,

A N D

Sir THOMAS DENISON, K^{nt}, one of his Majefty's Juftices, the 20th of *July*, 1752.

For the barbarous and inhuman Murder of JAMES WHALE, Husband of the faid ANNE WHALE, by Poifon, when ANNE WHALE was fentenced to be burnt, in being guilty of Petty Treafon.

And SARAH PLEDGE to be hanged, as being an Acceffary, Aider and Abettor in the faid Crime, which Sentence was accordingly executed on them on *Friday* the 7th of *Auguft* 1752, at *Horfham* aforefaid.

Together with their Authentick Examinations and Confeffions, taken before JOHN WICKER, and SAMUEL BLUNT, Efqrs, two of his Majefty's Juftices of the Peace for the County of *Suffex*.

This Pamphlet is worthy the Perufal of Perfons of all Ranks and Denominations, as it contains a Series of uncommon Events, and more particularly the remarkable Contrivance of *Sarah Pledge*, in endeavouring to poifon the faid *James Whale*, by putting Spiders in his Beer.

L O N D O N:

Printed for M. COOPER, at the *Globe* in *Pater-nofter Row*, and Meffrs. VERRAL and LEE, at *Lewes*.

[Price Six-Pence.]

This was a pamphlet sold in the streets of Horsham in the mid-eighteenth century. It claimed to be a genuine account of the murder by Anne Whale and Sarah Pledge of Anne's husband, and their subsequent execution on Horsham common. The unfortunate Anne was sentenced 'to be burned with fire until she be dead'. This was one of the last judicial executions by burning at the stake, although Widow Cruttenden was executed in a similar manner on Horsham Common in 1776. Tradition has it that Anne's screams could be heard as far away as Cidermill Farm, Warnham. However, the carrying out of the sentence was slightly less cruel than it appears, for the poor woman was strangled prior to the lighting of the fire. Horsham Common had long been a place of public merrymaking and entertainment, including the notorious Hang Fairs at which the main participant drew a large gathering of townsfolk, intent on an enjoyable day out. The pamphlet was typical of such publications which were produced and sold for a few pence on these occasions.

A public baptism conducted by Pastor C. Neal for the Horsham Baptist Union at Whitesbridge. This was on 17 April 1908 (Good Friday). The Baptist Union had been established in Horsham in 1894, with a service conducted in the King's Head Assembly Rooms in East Street. In 1897 an iron and brick chapel was opened in Brighton Road. This and other Baptist activity in Horsham came about following the repeal of the disabling Acts in 1828, and the Baptist faith spread rapidly.

The Entente Cordiale train passing the old Horsham West signal-box, *c.* 1905. It was taking the French Naval Fleet to London, following their arrival at Portsmouth, where they had been met and reviewed by Edward VII. The locomotive is No. 54 'Billinton', built in Brighton in 1900. Apparently it had three names: *Empress, Princess Royal* and, for one week only, *La France*. I suspect that train buffs may be able to add a lot more information.

Jury Cramp and other local dignitaries celebrating the completion of the fountain built on the Carfax in 1897, in honour of Queen Victoria's Diamond Jubilee. Diminutive Jury Cramp was well known in the town as an enthusiastic Temperance campaigner, so the water-fountain must have been particularly close to his heart. Other notables here include local landowners Robert Henry Hurst and William Lintott. The fountain was funded by public subscription. In 1947 it was removed, as it was said to be a hazard to traffic. It stayed in storage for thirty years until 1977, when the Horsham Museum Society and the Horsham Society had it re-erected in Copnall Way, to celebrate Queen Elizabeth's Silver Jubilee. When the Carfax was redesigned in 1994 the fountain was again moved; it has ended up in a very prominent position, at the point where North Street becomes a walkway to the Carfax.

USSEX COUNTY AGRICULTURAL SH

This is how the 25th Annual Sussex County Agricultural Show was advertised. It was held on the Horsham Show Ground adjoining Worthing Road from 12 to 13 July 1911. Admission tickets cost 1s, while a reserved seat in the grandstand cost the princely sum of 5s. This represented perhaps two days' work for many of our grandparents.

A view of the Sussex Agricultural Show at Horsham in July 1911. The programme included exhibitions of livestock and farm machinery, as well as displays by 'leading nurserymen in England'. For those with less agricultural tastes, there was an educational exhibition and cookery demonstrations. Music was provided by the full band of the 4th (Royal Irish) Dragoon Guards. One is struck by the similarity of the programme to present-day events of this kind, and it is pleasant to reflect that there are some things that have not changed too much in eighty years or so.

At the same show. Obviously this was a very important occasion for sleepy Horsham in the early years of this century. It was honoured with the presidency of Lord Leconfield, and the patronage of Earl Winterton, Horsham's MP. Tickets were sold by Price & Co., the local printers in West Street, who probably also did the printing work for the show. Other local traders must have found that these busy two days brought them some welcome extra business.

HORSHAM
Christmas Kissing Competition

(By Moonlight   By Special Desire).

CLUB   BADGE.

RULES.

**Competitors must bring 2 lips (Tulips).
Must be over 7 and under 70.
Onions and peppermints strictly prohibited.**
WILL YOU BE THERE?

A Kissing Competition in Horsham? If so I suppose I should have included it in the sports section. But although I have no information on this postcard, I think it was most likely a spoof. It probably dates from the First World War.

A postcard of Horsham Town Hall early this century. The original stone building was erected as an open market hall, with the upper part raised on arches. On assize days the arches were boarded up, to provide more rooms for the proceedings. In 1812 the Duke of Norfolk paid for extensive work to be done, and the building assumed its present appearance.

SECTION FOUR
Sporting Occasions

North Street decorated for Horsham Cricket Week, 1912. This was a popular annual event from 1908, continuing (with wartime breaks) until 1956. As well as the cricket itself, the programme included plays, dances, parties and concerts, and it provided an annual opportunity for local organizations to show off their activities, just as they do now in the Horsham Festival Week. The culmination of the week's merry-making was the carnival procession through the centre of the town. I can recall the thrill of waiting for the parade to reach my vantage-point and seeing the decorated floats, which were joined by the local services such as the fire brigade and the St John Ambulance. Then we all fell in behind the parade as it made its way into Horsham Park. The memory is of something magical.

West Street is seen here during the same Cricket Week. Later this street was to suffer the indignity of traffic being prohibited from moving first one way, and then the other, before finally becoming a pedestrian precinct. Note the horse manure on the road, something taken for granted in the days of the horse and cart. Not that its value as a garden aid was overlooked, as many otherwise staid townsfolk would lower their pride and dash out into the road at intervals, dustpan and brush at the ready. The many projecting shop signs here include the lovely pair of giant spectacle frames hanging from the upper storey of Jury Cramp's, jeweller's and optician's. This sign stayed in place until the business finally closed in 1986 and the familiar spectacles went to the museum.

Horsham's much loved cricket ground, pictured in the interwar years. The first recorded mention of cricket at Horsham was in 1768, although it was three years later before an actual game by a town side was noted. This was against High Chalvington. The original Horsham ground was in Denne Park, but Edward Tredcroft (who lived at the big house) gave the present ground to the town in 1851. This was the site of the old army barracks; in fact in my mother's time it was still usual to talk about 'walking to the Barrack Fields', rather than to the cricket ground. Horsham Cricket Club bought the site in the 1920s.

Horsham Cycling Club in the early 1900s. With the advent of the pneumatic tyre, cycling took off as one of the country's most popular recreations. Horsham's club began in 1908 in the Station Hotel, with forty-five keen founder members. The minutes of the club are now in the care of Horsham Museum, and they record such happy events as a race to Brighton, when members returned in time to attend the theatre. The museum also holds a solid silver cup made in Sheffield over fifty years ago which was presented to the winner of a race organized by the club, as well as many other documents, badges and certificates illustrating the club's history.

I believe this group is the Horsham Post Office Football Club team, pictured on the Horsham Football Ground in Queen Street, between the wars. Perhaps a reader can confirm or contradict this. The town's own football club was formed in 1870, and there have always been several other teams connected with firms or localities. For example, the Bishopric Club team and Trinity Football Club were great rivals. On one occasion the former carried a black coffin to represent Trinity, and the latter carried an effigy of a rook to signify the Bishopric, which had long been known as The Rookery.

A meeting of the Horsham Motor Cycle and Light Car Club on the Carfax, *c.* 1926. The popularity of sidecars at this time is very evident. The club was formed around 1921 and members enjoyed organized outings and treasure hunts, usually on a Sunday. One highlight was the Hill Trials, which were held with the ready cooperation of the police. These took place on Colgate Hill and Hurst Hill, with a policeman stationed at each end of the course and in telephone contact. Great fun, and very little other traffic around to bother them.

The Wealden Villages

An enchanting portrait of the Gardener family, 1901. Samuel (born in 1849) was the blacksmith at Southwater; his forge stood on the main road north of the village. Back row, left to right: Cecil, Aggie, Horace, May, Bert; middle row: Bessie, Samuel, his wife Fannie (born in 1851), Florrie; front row: Stan, Ethel, Minnie, Ella, Percy.

Southwater Cripplegate Windmill, before it was totally destroyed by a fire on 25 May 1914. By the time the Horsham fire engine arrived, it was nearly all over. The four horses required to pull the engine had to be fetched and the volunteers assembled; then there was the journey to Southwater, the horses almost worn out by the time they had galloped up Picts Hill.

The Hen and Chickens, one of the two Southwater inns, c. 1910. The landlady at that time was Mrs James Lewry, who is standing at the door with her dog; the gentleman is presumably her husband. Though unusual for pubs at that period, it stressed the fact that it also served teas. Although it seems a little unlikely, the pub is said to have been named after the Hen and Chickens Pentacycle, invented in Horsham by Mr Burstow in 1851. Recently a reproduction of the pentacycle, normally on display at Horsham Museum, was loaned to the pub when it was re-opened after modernization.

Stan Gardener (Samuel's son) had taken over his father's business by the 1930s, and the garage had completely replaced the blacksmith's forge. Car enthusiasts will probably drool over the car in the picture; interestingly the trade names are still thoroughly familiar. The bus in the background was probably one of Rayner's fleet, before its business was destroyed by fire, also in the 1930s.

Stan Gardener at the first petrol pump in Southwater in the 1930s. Stan had become a blacksmith by the time his father died, but he had bowed to the inevitable and moved over to motor cars and motor cycles by the time of this photograph. Now nothing remains of either the forge or the garage.

Southwater Village School in the 1920s. This was the classroom in the old school, built in 1844 and enlarged in 1888, and is very typical of its era. Included in the picture are Joyce Gardener, Jack Grinstead and Ronnie Charman (of Great House Farm). The wife of the headmaster is standing next to the globe at the back.

Maypole ribbon dancing at Southwater Flower Show, *c*. 1905. The lack of spectators is rather surprising as this type of maypole dancing became tremendously popular in Victorian times and has survived strongly to the present day. However, in spite of the 'olde English' appearance of the pinafored children, this is not really an English custom; it was imported from the Continent. Maypole dancing in medieval England was a much more virile and adult pastime.

These children appear to be carrying May Day garlands. They are posing in front of Southwater Village Hall around 1925. Although later than the photograph above, May Day garlands are a much earlier custom; they were very popular from the early nineteenth century or before, but in most places by the beginning of this century the custom was in decline. In this picture hats are very much in fashion, as are the rather heavy-looking upright cycles.

Schoolboys on drill parade at Southwater Village School, *c.* 1900. Mrs E. Davey was headmistress at about that time, but the picture has a very masculine look to it. The rifles are obviously replicas, but the helmets look surprisingly genuine.

A view of the main Horsham to Worthing road at Southwater, *c.* 1906. It is difficult to believe that this fairly narrow and decidedly muddy road was to become a busy main route to the coast, until it was bypassed in the 1970s. The road has been described as the longest village street in Sussex. In the centre of the photograph is a village shop, possibly that of James Burchett, who was the grocer and postmaster. The building was originally a pair of houses. The cart on the left appears to be making a delivery, as there is a barrel in the road (left corner).

Members of the Southwater Women's Institute, 1920s. (The first WI branch was formed in Sussex, at Singleton in 1915.) Included in this photograph are Mrs Polly, Mrs Gardener, Mrs Flint, Mrs Webster, Mrs Charman, Lady King, Mrs Hughes and Mrs Irvin. Again, it is quite obvious that no lady would venture out without a hat.

A very posed picture of the blacksmith's shop at Adversane, a small hamlet near Billingshurst. The picture is undated, but it is probably from the 1920s. The blacksmith here early this century was Alfred Taylor, although the best-known smith, who worked this forge between the wars, was Gaius Carley. He was born at Upper Dicker in 1888 and worked at Horsham and Kirdford on many different jobs, including bird scaring and stone picking. His first week in Adversane earned him 16s. The Adversane Fair was a particularly busy time, with many horses to be shod, the wheels of showman's vans to be repaired and work done on the ironwork of the many horse-drawn carts and vans.

The annual regatta on the river at Stopham on 24 July 1912. This was a popular event every summer held just beyond Stopham Bridge and was attended by most Pulborough folk and many from other villages. The boats on the water were attractively lit after dark, and there were other attractions such as a greasy pole across the water, and fireworks to conclude the proceedings.

Pulborough Market, 1920s. Most villages had their own markets at that time. At the turn of the century Pulborough had a market for corn each Friday near the Swan Hotel, and a market for livestock on alternate Mondays. There was also an annual fair for toys and pedlars on Easter Tuesday. Mrs Winifred Cousins recalled: 'You could buy almost anything in Pulborough Market. Some stallholders came from London, and there was always good butter, poultry and eggs.' The market area is now used as a car park.

These cottages at the bottom of Church Hill, Pulborough, are believed to be the oldest in the village. There is an old Tudor chimney at one end, and some of the beams are said to come from ships. Under the building is a cellar, which, so tradition has it, was used as a cock-fighting pit. This fine view is from around 1890, when D.W. Dilloway, saddler and harness maker, was in business here. By 1903 his widow Mrs Mary Dilloway was running the shop, with Mr Orford as manager. Mr Orford later bought the business from her. The shop subsequently became a greengrocer's, then a florist's and finally a hairdresser's.

Pulborough Whit Monday Carnival. The picture is undated, but the first of these events was held in 1931, so this was probably soon after that date. This particular float, with the participants in attractive costumes, appears to represent the people of the British Isles. There is a Welsh lady with her harp, a very Irish-looking 'character', a Highlander and presumably an 'English Rose'. In the centre is the figure of Britannia.

Pulborough Hockey Team, *c.* 1917. The lack of male players is notable. Although I have been unable to track down any specific information on the team, it is obvious that Pulborough was always very active in sports, including football, cricket, stoolball and bowling.

A haystack fire at Lloyt's Farm, Partridge Green, *c.* 1906. Apparently five ricks caught fire that night, and the risk of such an occurrence caused constant anxiety to the farmers. The fires were attended by the volunteer fire brigades from both Horsham and Henfield. The bearded gentleman (far left) is George Arthur Gates, the owner of Lloyt's Farm and also Copyhold Farm.

Mr Philip Kensett of Partridge Green with his horse and trap, *c.* 1914. He was listed in a local directory as a horse dealer, although here he appears to be delivering bread. On the back of the photograph it is revealed that 'this mare cost £40. Bought Barnett Fair. 14 years ago. 14 hands. Still delivers bread.'

A rather genteel-looking group packing strawberries in Partridge Green, *c.* 1913.

St George's Church, West Grinstead, *c.* 1920. It is difficult to determine why the church was built here, as there is really no village to speak of. To the south runs the river, which was once busy with barges. Tradition says that the Knights Templars from Shipley used the river, and it is likely that local people also made use of it to come to church. At the end of the sixteenth century it was recorded that 'the church [was] very much default, especially the roof, whereby it raineth down'. But from the seventeenth century the building was kept in good repair, and there was a major restoration in 1890.

The secret chapel and some of its relics in the Priest's House, West Grinstead; the photograph probably dates from the 1920s. The chapel is a famous Roman Catholic shrine, visited by pilgrims from all over the world. It has been altered over the years to allow easy access; during post-Reformation times it was probably reached via a priest's hiding-hole. It is said that one day there were as many as a dozen priests together in the house when searchers came looking for them. One brave priest walked out to the front garden and gave himself up for the sake of the others. So elated were the hunters that they forgot to continue their search, and the rest escaped the immediate danger.

The Burrell Arms, West Grinstead, early this century. The plain-looking inn was on the main road and I remember it from my childhood as a popular bus-stop for the No. 2 Southdown on its way to Worthing. William Sherlock was the landlord at about the time of this photograph. The inn was named in honour of the local Burrell family, who played a considerable part in public life. Sir Merrik Burrel MP obtained his baronetcy for his services as Governor of the Bank of England. He bought West Grinstead Park from the Caryll family in 1750. His nephew William was a great collector who helped to lay the foundations of Sussex historical research. William lived at Knepp Castle in the nearby parish of Shipley.

Cyclists' Rest, West Grinstead. In the early 1900s this was a grocer's shop and was a useful stopping-place for cyclists at the time when the cycling craze was sweeping the country.

May Day garlands at Cowfold, 1911. Mr T. Mills, the owner of this photograph, is the solemn-looking young man on the right. By this time the charming custom of May garlands was waning and a contemporary newspaper commented: 'This was a revival of the good old times at Cowfold on May Day. The joyous customs which in the past heralded the happy month of May have been allowed to get into a state of desuetude, but thanks to the kindliness of Mr J.H. Pitcher, a change has come over the scene.' This gentleman's 'kindliness' took the form of prizes totalling 10s, for the children who produced the best garlands: the May queen received 3s 6d and there were two oranges for each competitor. In addition Mrs H. Gander gave each child 1d and Miss C.E. Vinall contributed a bag of biscuits.

A hat-trimming competition, probably part of a fête or garden party, held in Cowfold, *c*. 1920. The male competitors seen here are surprisingly unembarrassed by the photographer. The lady's hat (far right), though apparently not part of the contest, would certainly have merited first prize.

The Carthusian Monastery known as St Hugh's Charterhouse was founded at Parkminster (near Cowfold) in 1873, after the monks had been expelled from France. Building started in 1876, with almost seven hundred workmen of various nationalities. In 1883 the first prior was appointed and the church was consecrated. After three centuries the rule of monastic life, which had been extinguished at the Reformation, was re-established in this country. The buildings were designed to house eighty monks and thirty lay brothers, although there are now far fewer. Pictured here, on either side of the main doorway, are statues of St John the Baptist, patron saint of the solitary life, and St Bruno, founder of the order. These are being repainted in 1994. The building is seen here around 1907, though it still looks the same today.

Billingshurst celebrating the coronation of George V on 28 June 1911. The population of Billingshurst at that time was about two thousand. It was a busy little village on the old Roman road, seven miles from Horsham, and there was a carrier who travelled to and from Horsham six days a week – a most important and useful person. One of the commonest names in the village was Wadey; different members of the family were wheelwrights, builders, undertakers and even tax collectors.

Billingshurst railway station and staff (plus dog), 1900. There was no shortage of help at that time, even for a small station. Walter Simmons was the stationmaster around that time, so presumably he is the bearded gentleman standing behind the dog. Billingshurst was the first station south of Horsham and came into existence when the Mid-Sussex Railway Company (formed in 1857) built a line from Horsham to Pulborough.

Christ's Hospital railway station, looking north towards Horsham. The station was opened in 1902 when the Bluecoat School moved from London to the Sussex countryside. This was a vast station for such a rural position, owing to the large number of pupils expected to use it daily. But too late it was decided that the school would cater for boarders only, so the huge platforms were not needed, except at the beginning and end of term. The Guildford branch platform can be seen on the left. Now only part of the station is still in use, though it had a brief moment of fame when it was featured in the film *Rotten to the Core* as 'Longhampton'.

Motley Fair at Jolesfield House, near Partridge Green. The picture is undated, but it appears to date from early this century. This is obviously not a fair in the usual sense of the word, but more a fête provided by the 'Big House'. The owner of Jolesfield House at that time was Robert John Frank, so he could be the dapper man with the beard (centre, right). Note the interesting selection of outfits and hats, including a group at the back wearing seaside-type pierrot costumes. The local Boy Scouts are also in attendance on the right. Unfortunately there is no indication on the picture as to the identity of the lady (centre, left), who is possibly making an opening speech.

Barns Green post office and stores, *c.* 1900. The shop was run by Mrs Maria Peskett and was also a grocer's and draper's. It served a population of about five hundred, and as this picture shows it was a busy store. It stood next to the Queen's Head, in which Barns Green Friendly Society, a village club, assembled. The club also held its annual celebrations there on the third Monday in July. Described as 'the biggest day in the year', there was a procession led by a man in a white smock, followed by the local band. Afrer a service in the church, there was lunch in a big marquee and a fair on the green.

The Swan at Fittleworth, *c.* 1905. Its famous arch (centre) bore the shields of the Duke of Norfolk and Lord Leconfield. Tradition says that on the back of the original inn sign was a naked lady, with features resembling Queen Victoria. The lady's features were changed and her nudity partially covered with veiling. The inn, which stands near the Arun, has always been well loved by all who stay there, including authors, artists (such as Constable), and of course anglers. The sending of the postcard has really written the caption for me: 'If you want apartments at any time, this is the place to go. Nice Lover's Walk and every accommodation.'

The interior of the watermill at Coolham, Easter 1915. The rather solemn-looking boys were, I am sure, very pleased to be in the photograph. The mill was probably the one at Slaughter Bridge. The parish of Shipley, in which Coolham lies, once had several windmills and watermills.

The George and Dragon at Dragons Green, Shipley, *c.* 1912. The name is traditionally thought to refer to the dragon legends in this part of Sussex, although it may well have had a more prosaic origin. On the far right is the memorial to Walter Budd, who lived in the pub with his parents, and who drowned himself in 1893, when he was just twenty-six.

SECTION SIX

The Border Villages

The Church Army at Slinfold around 1904, seemingly determined not to let the Salvation Army have all the action. This is the No. 1 van from Chichester together with a mainly youthful audience, all apparently in their Sunday best. The message on the back of the postcard says: 'I thought you would like this one better than the sheep.' I hope the recipient was as charmed with the picture as I was when I first saw it.

Slinfold's oldest inhabitant around 1890. I do not know anything about this lady, but it seems that they live to a good age in this village. In 1922 the oldest inhabitant was Phil Parker, and he had been a corporal in Her Majesty's 55th Regiment of Foot in the Crimean War. In 1919 the *Daily Mail* reported that one of the oldest men in the village at that time had said that he had one regret: that he had never been in a flying machine. His companion, who was nearly as old, replied in all seriousness, 'No, but many's the time I've ridden in a broad-wheeled wagon.'

Frank Wadey & Sons, wheelwrights and blacksmiths, at their forge in The Street, Slinfold, opposite the Congregational Church, around 1886. (The main street in Slinfold has always been called simply The Street.) The young lad with the interesting hat is Edward Venn, a fourteen-year-old apprentice. The lady in the background (left) evidently wanted to get into the picture.

Slinfold station, *c*. 1910. It was operated by the London Brighton & South Coast Railway company and was situated half a mile south of the village, on the old Horsham to Guildford line. It opened in 1865 and closed under the Beeching axe a century later. In 1903 Harry Raggett was the stationmaster, so this is probably him pictured with his little daughter. The station had three signal-boxes, a goods yard and crane, and three private sidings – all these facilities reflected the industries of the area, including hoop making, charcoal burning, a tanyard, brickworks, basket factory and timber yard.

Slinfold village, with the Child Memorial Hall in the background (left), *c*. 1910. Slinfold has always attracted compliments. Nairn and Pevsner, in *The Buildings of England*, describe it as 'Leafy Weald, slightly rolling and beautifully cared for'. In 1919 a national newspaper said it was 'at the end of nowhere' but conceded that it was 'a little heaven on earth'. They claimed to have discovered a farmer who 'rises at four every morning, brews his own beer, and knows his sheep and cattle as well as he knows his men'.

The beginning of mechanization on the farms: steam threshing at Holmbush Farm, Slinfold, in 1910. It was obviously significant enough for a photographer to travel out from Horsham to capture the event. Youngsters have always embraced new-fangled things rather more readily than their elders; one who remembered the gangs which travelled with the steam threshing outfits recalled how he envied those devil-may-care men as they handled the steam monsters with ease and appeared to be afraid of nothing.

Slinfold, *c.* 1910. This was a busy village, whose industries included stone quarrying. It was one of the places where the famous Horsham slabs were quarried, to be taken by river to the sea. Now there are no more slabs to be quarried, and the Horsham Stone that remains is prized.

A typical farming scene at Slinfold, *c.* 1900. There were several local farms, and this is believed to be Old House Farm, which was owned by Mrs Mary Boniface. Although there were a number of other industries at Slinfold, undoubtedly the largest proportion of the males, out of a population of around a thousand, would have been employed in agricultural work. A guide book of the period states that wheat, oats and turnips were the chief crops.

A funeral picture with a degree of mystery attached to it. It has been described to me as a funeral at Slinfold around 1912, with the mourners leaving Barrack Cottages, headed by Mr Thomas Ayling, the local undertaker and builder. However, I have been told elsewhere that it was a Cokeler's funeral at Loxwood, at around the same time. The mourners look as if they might be members of the religious sect, the Christian Dependents (popularly known as Cokelers), but the flowers on the bier are completely out of character with their philosophy. I would love to know more about this picture, if any reader can oblige.

Rudgwick Upper Smithy, on the main road through Bucks Green, early 1900s. The blacksmith was William Meeten, who was described as a shoeing and general smith. This was across the road from the popular Queen's Head, so it was a great place for the village men, with time on their hands, to meet, smoke their pipes and talk. There was always something to watch and a fire to warm them in the winter. The horse and trap in the foreground may belong to the village doctor, Frank Boxall, who used this form of conveyance to visit his patients – at least until he succumbed to the new-fangled motor car.

Rudgwick station in the late nineteenth century. This was also on the London Brighton & South Coast line from Horsham to Guildford. The stationmaster was Louis Arthur Brighty and he is probably the figure to the left. Among the fine examples of Victorian fashions is a young lad in a sailor suit (right). There was also a busy goods yard here, and it was said that more boxes of mushrooms than passengers were sent out by train. The station opened a little later than the others on this line, but closed in 1965 after serving the village for about a hundred years. Before the arrival of the trains, the only way to get to Horsham was on foot.

Charlie Woodhatch was a well-known figure in Rudgwick in the early 1900s. He worked as gardener for Mrs Cooper at Highcroft. Note the use of the scythe, which points to Mr Woodhatch being a gardener of the old-fashioned kind.

Ivy Cottage (now renamed Two Wells), Rudgwick, *c.* 1903. The group around the shop (with the canopy) has been identified as Mr Edwin Edmunds, who was the grocer and assisant overseer, plus three ladies with the names Manders, Flemings and Laudets.

The Old Toll House, next to the forge, on the main road at Bucks Green, *c.* 1908. Mr and Mrs Merritt lived in the house at that time, and possibly Mrs Merritt is the figure on the far right. She is remembered as a lady who carried water from the well, with a yoke on her shoulders.

Rudgwick Church of the Holy Trinity. The photograph is undated but is probably from early this century. To the right is the vicarage and in the foreground is Mr Dewdney's baker's cart on its rounds. The church, was largely rebuilt in the fourteenth century, and has been described as 'wide, high and spacious'. There are several legends attached to it. One is of the Rudgwick Bell, which was being transported to the church and slipped into a bog near Roman Gate. Many attempts were made to rescue it, but the Evil One frustrated all the efforts, even in the 1970s when a dowser was employed. There is also the tale of a tunnel, which is supposed to run from the King's Head to the church and probably dates from smuggling days.

Rudgwick Sanatorium for Consumption, or The Sanatorium as it was normally called, c. 1906. The proprietor was Miss Annie McCall. Local children would always run past the building as fast as they could, afraid of what the consequences might be if they lingered. The patients seen here with their nurses have not been evacuated for a fire drill; this was all part of the treatment, which was based largely on as much fresh air as possible, hence the wide open windows.

The old cottage on the main road at Bucks Green, *c.* 1900. It was once called Snoxalls, but more recently was known as Goblins Pool. By that time it looked a little smarter than in this photograph. I have many memories of the building in its Goblins Pool days, many involved with not remembering to duck my head when passing into the additional section on the right. The two young children in this picture are twins, Alfred and Winifred Chasemore.

Kirdford School, *c.* 1910. This was originally built in 1819 and enlarged in 1898 to take 153 pupils (or scholars as they were always called at that time). The master and mistress of the school were Mr Jesse and Mrs Elizabeth Goodacre. They were probably very proud of their girls in their white pinafores. Some idea of the conditions of schools at the turn of the century can be gained from an inspector's report on Plaistow School in the same parish: 'The cess-pool is not properly covered in. The infants are in good order, but separation by a curtain might be useful, as there is no classroom.'

The Half Moon, opposite the church at Kirdford, early this century. The inn sign is inscribed with the name Pelham, the landlord at that time. It was once common to place the licensee's name on the sign, rather than that of the pub itself, and in Kirdford people talked about 'going to Pelham's' rather than 'going to the Half Moon'. Mrs D. Treadwell of Kirdford recalled when her grandparents had the Half Moon, around 1905. The farmers came to church in their traps, and left her father to put their horses in the inn stables. The drovers with their Kent sheep stopped in the village on their way home, and her grandmother provided lunch for them in the clubroom.

Kirdford village, c. 1910. It has always been a somewhat old-fashioned place and is very proud of its history. I am told that even people who came to live here from other counties were considered 'foreigners'. Two of the main industries in this part of Sussex are glass making and fruit growing, and there is a happy tradition of wassailing the fruit trees at the new year. This has been carried on in modern times by local morris men.

Kirdford post office, *c.* 1910. The postmaster at this time was Mr Percy Ford, and letters were received from Billingshurst twice a day. (There were even two deliveries on Sundays.) This and the other pictures of Kirdford came from a cache of old glass plates found in an attic by my father, many years ago.

Wisborough Green post office, early 1900s. Mrs Emma Wadey was sub-postmistress at about that time. As at Kirdford, letters came from Billingshurst twice daily. The cottage next to the post office appears to be empty and has a 'For Sale' board in the front garden. The village pond, complete with ducks, is in the foreground.

Loxwood, which is situated on the Surrey border, early this century. On the left is Blackwool (later known as Black Hall), and next to it is the old forge. In 1903 Benjamin Luff was the blacksmith, and he is probably the figure standing in the doorway. He may have lived in the house – although it does look a trifle grand.

The Cokeler's chapel, built in 1870, at Loxwood. The origins of this chapel read more like a legend than a true story. John Sirgood was born in Gloucestershire in 1820. In 1850 he was told in a dream of a village in Sussex which needed him. The next day he closed his shoemaker's shop and, with his wife in a barrow (like St Cuthman and his mother in a cart), he set out on the 40 mile trip from London to Loxwood. To begin with, only five people joined this itinerent preacher, but within ten years half the village were his disciples.

SECTION SEVEN

The Northern Villages

A splendid sight: haymakers at Warnham, *c.* 1914. The site is thought to be Warnham Lodge, the seat of Sir Henry Harben, who was a local JP. The size of the workforce gives some idea of how such things have changed since the days when labour was cheap and farms were the biggest employers in the countryside. In many villages agriculture was almost the only occupation open to a lad when he left school. However some villages offered alternatives, particularly when the railway age began. In Warnham there was also the brickworks, where, as in farming, work was hard and long.

Warnham Watermill, *c.* 1900. Nearer to Horsham than Warnham village, it is still in existence and has changed very little. Although the building is now used as offices, the mill wheel and its mechanism were rebuilt in 1985, and sometimes the splendid sight and sound of the wheel working may still be experienced. My grandfather is reputed to have worked in this mill as a young man. Sadly, there was no work for a miller in the later years of his life, and he ended his working days as a gardener. My father recalled playing with his friends around the mill – play which, I suspect, would have been forbidden in these more safety-conscious times.

Warnham Millpond, as seen from a plane of Surrey Flying Services operating from Croydon Airport, probably in the 1920s. The wing of the plane can be seen on the left. The fine vista of the countryside around the pond shows very few buildings. The millpond was originally a hammer pond, in the days of the Sussex ironworks. It was owned by Charles Lucas, but is now part of a nature reserve cared for by the Horsham District Council.

Warnham Millpond, November 1906. It is seen here after the floodgates, built in 1876, had given way, draining the pond. Many pictures were taken at that time, including some showing the masses of fish which were left stranded. These conditions have revealed the stream which runs through the centre of the pond, and which could cause dangerous situations to develop when the pond was frozen. The little girl being held firmly by her hands is evidently being shown a sight which she might never experience again.

The Sussex Oak, Warnham, early this century. Originally it was known simply as The Oak, and it is one of the two village pubs which still exist; the other is The Greets. Part of the Sussex Oak is Georgian and it is also partly Victorian; it has lots of oak beams and open fireplaces. A 1903 directory lists E. Hammond as the landlord and James Baker as fly proprietor, Sussex Oak Stables. The pub is opposite the parish church of St Margaret, which has an arch of yew trees instead of a conventional lych-gate. The area in front of the pub was once the site for bonfires on 5 November, as well as an annual visit by a travelling circus.

The first Warnham Flower Show, 30 August 1906. It was held in the grounds of Warnham Court, the seat of Lt.-Col. Charles Lucas, JP, and was the beginning of a tradition of such shows, considered to be some of the best in the county.

Warnham String Band, photographed on 9 April 1910. The band, which in spite of its title was certainly not composed entirely of string players, was first mentioned in village records in March 1908. The first concert was on 30 December 1909 and the last account is of a rehearsal in January 1914. Back row, left to right: E. Chennell, Arthur Charman (conductor), C. Kemp; middle row: A.C. Yates, F. Francis, Alec Edwards, F. Edwards, A. Harding, T. Burridge, Albert Charman; front row: Miss L. Edwards, Miss M. Foster, Miss N. Hamond, Miss F. Branch, A. Goring, Peter Charman. The child seated at the front is Nellie Burrage, aged nine.

The Warnham village stocks, 1935. Most places in Sussex had stocks for minor crimes, although many of them have now disappeared. Some were even burnt on 5 November bonfires as they were no longer in use. Other places have produced replicas, but Warnham's stocks appear to be the genuine article. Apparently they were once housed inside the church and later outside the village hall.

A bazaar, probably what we would call a fête, in the grounds of Warnham Court, the home of the Lucas family. There were fine grounds here with ponds, fountains, summerhouses, greenhouses and statues. The lady on the right is Lady Harben, wife of Sir Henry Harben of Warnham Lodge. It is difficult to make out what display the well-dressed ladies are looking at, but it appears to be something quite elaborate.

Warnham Millpond, frozen over in February 1911. Note the singular uniforms of the boys from Christ's Hospital School on the left. In my childhood the pond seemed to freeze each winter, and although I was never allowed to try skating, my father would take me there to watch and, if I was lucky, enjoy some of the chestnuts being roasted on the bank. There were tragedies, however, and this led to skating being forbidden in more recent times. Warnham Millpond was one of the few places from his childhood which the poet Shelley referred to in his writings.

Mr F.W. Freeman's shop in Church Street, Warnham, *c.* 1906. He was a very well-known and respected local tradesman, who lived in the house next to his shops. As well as selling provisions and meat, he was the Warnham Postmaster, President of the Grocers Association, churchwarden and a member of the church choir. Also seen here (with the horse and cart) is Mr Frederick Branch, who had a baker's shop in School Hill. Of the group in white aprons, the man on the left is probably James Packham, Mr Freeman is in the middle and Mr Jupp is on the right. The man in front of the butcher's (right) is Mr Budgen. The postman and the man on the horse are so far unidentified, but perhaps a reader will be able to help.

A reminder of the early days of aviation in Sussex. Mr Barber in his flying machine *Valkyrie* made a forced landing at Warnham, due to a broken wing, on 1 August 1911. This was not the only time that planes landed or took off from the Horsham area in those early days of flying. Mr Elliott, who was one of the four sons of a Horsham grocer, ran a flying school at Shoreham, and there are several postcards showing his biplane taking off from Broadbridge Heath. Another card from the same period shows a Mr Valentine making a descent at Horsham on 4 August 1911, so, in view of the dates, presumably he had some connection with Mr Barber.

A well-known Warnham character – Mr Charman, the sexton, is seated on a tomb outside St Margaret's Church, 1905. He was evidently a favourite of the photographers, as another picture of him in the church doorway appeared as a Christmas card in the same year. He was succeeded as sexton by his son-in-law, Mr Etherton. Another renowned Warnham character was Michael Turner, the parish clerk and musician, who died in 1885. Sometimes postcards of Mr Charman are incorrectly captioned as Michael Turner.

The Wheatsheaf Hotel at Kingsfold, c. 1920. The proprietor was T. Williams. This was the heyday of the motor charabancs, with day trips in summer and evening mystery tours. This is quite a busy scene, so the Nigger Minstrels on the left were probably doing good business. Kingsfold was also famous for a very different type of music. It was here that the composer Ralph Vaughan Williams heard the folk-song 'The Red Barn' and was so impressed by the tune that he renamed it 'Kingsfold' and used it for the hymn 'I Heard the Voice of Jesus Say'. One way of making certain that the Devil didn't have all the best tunes.

Warnham village school, *c.* 1900. This was built in 1872 for 200 children, but had an average attendance of 175. In 1903 Thomas Stroud was the headmaster and Miss Carolyne Lloyd was in charge of the infants. In schools at that time, the infants were taught separately from the rest of the 'scholars', although sometimes they were expected to work in just a corner of the main classroom. Discipline was harsh by modern standards, and there was poor heating and very basic sanitation. But most of the teachers were dedicated, and the adults usually looked back with affection at their school days.

The scene at Broadbridge Heath when a car overturned, on Saturday 9 July 1910. Motor accidents were taken very seriously in those early days and any incident of this sort was thought worthy of a postcard; in fact this was labelled photo no. 1 so there were evidently others taken of the same accident. It was even thought worthwhile producing a card showing the empty road, where the accident had taken place. Perhaps it was as well that none of the people present at this accident in 1910 could see into the future. By 1920 it was recorded in the Broadbridge Heath School logbook: '. . . is absent today having been knocked over by a motor car'; so the age of the car with all its advantages and disadvantages had begun.

The creeper-covered village hall, or parish room as it was sometimes known, at Broadbridge Heath, c. 1908. It had a relatively short life, having been built early this century and ending its useful life by the 1930s. Village halls of this kind were invaluable, making it possible to hold every kind of event from pantomimes to film shows. Until such halls appeared, the church was perhaps the only building in the village capable of holding a reasonable number of people, and most have been built and maintained by the hard work and dedication of the villagers themselves.

Foster's Cottages in Broadbridge Heath were typical of much living accommodation in the nineteenth century. Even for clean and thrifty housewives the household conditions would have been less than ideal, with outdoor sanitation and water to be fetched from a well. Mr Thomas Foster was a landowner and poultry breeder at around that time, so presumably these cottages were owned by him. Some idea of the difficulties of working folk in the late 1800s may be gleaned from these two extracts from the Broadbridge Heath School logbooks of the time. From 1874: 'Sent G. and F. Knight home to be washed.' From 1875: 'A. Wood sent home for her school money, and she did not return. Mrs Wood sent rude message about it.'

What were described as the New Post Office Cottages, in Broadbridge Heath, c. 1910. Mrs Jane Richardson was the sub-postmistress around that time, but as far as I can discover the cottages had no actual connection with the post office; they were merely built in the vicinity. They look surprisingly modern and well built, and no doubt large families were very happy to move into buildings like this, rather than the typical older accommodation, which lacked indoor water and sanitation.

The blacksmith's workshop at Broadbridge Heath, early this century. Postcard photographers liked nothing better than to take a picture of the village smithy. With this one he had the perfect caption: 'Under the spreading Chestnut-tree.' The smith at about that time was Alfred Goring. It may be him standing behind the cartwheel, and perhaps also his wife and daughter. Or were they extras imported by the photographer to improve the composition?

Field Place, near Broadbridge Heath and one mile south-west of Warnham; a peaceful view from the early 1900s. Original parts of the building probably date back to the fifteenth century, with additions in the seventeenth. Other changes were made in 1846 and in 1931. This was the birthplace of Percy Bysshe Shelley, and it was in this tranquil spot that he spent his childhood. Although he appears to have enjoyed the countryside around the house, it did not hold his affection in later life. He returned in 1815 for the funeral of his grandfather, but was refused admission. This conjures up a poignant picture of the young poet, sitting forlornly outside his original home, unwelcome and unwanted.

The entrance to Roffey Camp. The message on the reverse of the card reads: 'This is where I am doing my Guard.' As well as the Fusiliers, at other times there were Canadians from Prince Edward Island and 1,300 Portuguese stationed there. One day the latter mutineered and the officers hid themselves and sent for the local Roman Catholic priest, Fr Bernard Cassidy. Meanwhile the Portuguese had climbed the trees in the camp, and it took all Father Cassidy's powers of persuasion to get them to come down. Hearing that Territorials had been summoned from Crowborough, they agreed to behave, and were sent off to France.

Crawley Road, close to Roffey Corner, c. 1908. The pub is the White Horse, affectionately known as The Pony. On the left is the coachman from Roffey Park House, a mansion built in the traditional style on an estate formerly owned by the Duke of Norfolk. Much of the carved panelling in the house came from the older Roughey Place, nearby. In the 1960s Roffey Park became a rehabilitation centre for patients recovering from illness, and my own very pleasant memories of it concern playing in the band for the weekly barn dances held in the ballroom.

St Andrew's, Roffey Methodist Church, photographed before the present porch had been added, c. 1937. The church was built in 1877 and was originally known as the Roffey Primitive Methodist Chapel. This was before the Methodist Union of 1932 brought both wings of the Methodist Church together.

The gnome-like Jury Cramp, well-known Horsham Temperance reformer and local jeweller, laying the final brick for the completion of the vestry extension at Roffey (St Andrew's) Methodist Church in 1937. Mr Cramp, who had been born in 1846, was a real Horsham character and was loved for his eccentricities. Note the wonderful ear-trumpet which he is holding in his left hand.

Crawley Road, Roffey, *c.* 1937. Why the photographer should have thought it worthwhile including King & Chasemore's advertising boards on a postcard is difficult to imagine. Just out of sight to the right is the Star public house, which folklore maintains had its doorstep exactly on a level with the top of the spire of St Mark's Church, down the hill in Horsham. The Star smock mill was near this part of Roffey, known as Star Row. Just visible between the telegraph poles is the last surviving toll house in the Horsham area; it was not demolished until 1946. When the wind blew particularly strongly across the Carfax, it was often remarked that the Star toll gate in Roffey had been left open.

Another view of Crawley Road, *c.* 1908. At that time Roffey was referred to as a place 'where nothing ever happens'. This contrasts with another description slightly later, 'Red Roffey', which evidently referred to its politics; although to call any part of Sussex 'red' at that time must have been something of an exaggeration. The population of Roffey in 1907 was given as 1,200. It was considered a bad route into Horsham, although at the same time the air was said to be healthier than in the town. Cobbett did not enjoy his ride into Horsham from Crawley, calling it 'six of the worst miles in England' and 'a most villainous tract'. Poor old Roffey never had a particularly good press, although when I was at school there in the 1930s it always seemed a very friendly place.

The Dun Horse, Mannings Heath, *c.* 1914. This building was demolished in the 1920s and a new Dun Horse built. As this lively picture shows, it must have been the hub of village life. As well as the pub, there was a butcher's and provision shop at one end of the building, and I am told that this stayed open until 11 p.m. on Saturdays. Another memory of the pub is of the cellars being flooded in the winter months and the problems this caused.

The Grapes at Peas Pottage, *c.* 1900. The pub is still there today. The cart (left) was owned by Arthur William Arnold, the miller from Roffey – Arnold is a common surname in the area. Occasionally the messages on the back of these old postcards are as interesting as the views. This unsigned one, says: 'The photo is of the cart Dad used to drive. He is in the House having his dinner (not drinking, as he never drunk anything intoxicating).' Evidently he had no intention of being caught 'Drunk in charge of a horse and cart', which was an accusation sometimes brought in the courts at that time.

St Saviour's Church at Colgate, 1908. It had been consecrated on 22 November 1871, and incorporated the old chapel, which had been in occasional use and which stood on the site of the present porch. The little church cost just over £1,800 and was built with financial help from local people and the vicars of Upper and Lower Beeding. Colonel J.C. Brown designed the building and his descendants donated the pulpit and lectern in 1925.

Holmbush Tower at Colgate. Our ancestors loved towers and follies; some of them had a definite purpose, while others were built merely to add interest to the local skyline. This attractive building dated from 1855 and was constructed largely from local stone. It was said tht Mr Sumner, who built it, laid every stone himself, although he had a lad to help him. The tower was stated to be 100 ft high and 570 ft above the level of high tide at London Bridge. In the days when a Sunday afternoon cycle ride was the highlight of the week, youngsters would pedal out from Horsham, paying 3d to climb the tower, and enjoying a glass of lemonade after their descent. The tower no longer exists, having been removed sometime during the Second World War, although not before the Home Guard had made use of it.

A typical view of St Leonard's Forest in the early 1900s. The forest is well known for its folklore and legends, although William Cobbett failed to see the romance of it. He talked of 'bare heath, with here and there some scrubby birch'. In 1794 Arthur Young described it as 'an extensive tract of waste land, producing nothing but rabbits'. Earlier still it had been part of the 'Black Country' of Sussex, producing iron for the Romans and again from the fourteenth century onwards.

An idyllic view of St Leonard's Forest, c. 1914. One of the legends for which the forest is noted concerns the Sussex Serpent; references to this often appeared from the seventeenth century onwards. It was in 1614 that a pamphlet appeared, purporting to be a true account of a large dragon or serpent witnessed by several local people in the forest. Cynics sometimes suggest that many of these old tales originated with the smugglers, who were most anxious to keep prying eyes away from their illegal night-time activities.

Bibliography

Albery, W.: *A Millenium of Facts in the History of Horsham and Sussex*, 1947.
Baldwin, M.: *The Story of the Forest*, 1971.
Bayley, C.H.: *Ifold, Loxwood and Plaistow*, 1988.
Brunnarius, M.: *The Windmills of Sussex*, 1979.
Burstow, H.: *Reminiscences of Horsham*, 1911.
Chapman, B.: *West Sussex Inns*, 1988.
Fryer, N.: *Natural History of St Leonard's Forest*, 1983.
Hill, A.: *The Family Fortune*, 1978.
Holmes, F.: *In and Around Horsham*, 1987.
——: *Horsham Town and Country Stories*, 1990.
——: *Stories of Old Horsham*, (undated).
Hudson, T.P.: *A History of Horsham*, 1986.
Hurst, D.: *Horsham: It's History and Antiquities*, 1868 and 1889.
Marley, T.A.: *A History of the Village of Slinfold*, 1975.
Mitchell, V. and Smith, K.: *Branch Lines to Horsham*, 1982.
Muggeridge, R.: *Warnham: A History*, 1985.
Nairn, I. and Pevsner, N.: *The Buildings of England: Sussex*, 1965.
Neale, K.: *Victorian Horsham*, 1975.
Turner, J.T.H.: *The London, Brighton and South Coast Railway*. Vols 1, 2, 3, 1977, 1978, 1979.
Walker, P.: *Rudgwick Memories*, 1982.
Walker, R.L.: *Sussex Pubs*, 1966.
Walser: *Illustrated Guide to Horsham and District*, 1892.
West Sussex County Times
West Sussex Gazette
Winbolt, S.E.: *History of the Parish Church of St Mary the Virgin, Horsham*, 1941.
Windrum, A.: *Horsham.: An Historical Survey*, 1978.
Windrum, A. and Hughes, A.: *Bygone Horsham*, 1982.

Acknowledgements

First I must record my special thanks to Mr C.W. Cramp and Mr J. Cannon for the exceptional help they have given me in the compilation of this book, both regarding the loan of pictures and in providing me with information. I would also like to acknowledge my debt to those who have given or lent me pictures, and also in many cases provided valuable information on them:

Mrs V. Blake • the Misses Boxall • Mr R. Charman • Mrs J. Coleman
Mrs W. Cousins • Mr and Mrs D. Harmsworth • Mr F. Holmes • Mrs Howard
Mrs J. Ilsley • Lens of Sutton • Mr T. Mills • Mr J. Muggeridge • Mr and Mrs J. Payne
Mrs J. Robertson • Mrs D. Treadwell • Mr F. Venn • Mrs E.D. Vincent • Mrs C. Wales
Mr D.Y. Young of Christ's Hospital School

A special thank you to David Turner and Fran Broad, who helped me so much with the preparation of many of the photographs. And of course my late father and mother, who shared so many of their memories with me. My sincere apologies to anyone who should have been included, but whom I have unintentionally omitted.